Faces of God

Gordon and Gladis DePree

THE WESTMINSTER PRESS
Philadelphia

The Scripture quotations in this publication are from the following versions:

Good News for Modern Man, the New Testament in Today's English Version (TEV), © American Bible Society 1966, 1971.

The Holy Bible, Authorized King James Version (KJV).

The New English Bible (NEB), © The Delegates of the Oxford University Press and The Syndics of the Cambridge University Press 1961, 1970.

The Revised Standard Version Bible (RSV), copyrighted 1946 (renewed 1973), 1952 and © 1971 by the Division of Christian Education of the National Council of the Churches of Christ in the U.S.A.

Published by The Westminster Press®
Philadelphia, Pennsylvania

PRINTED IN THE UNITED STATES OF AMERICA
9 8 7 6 5 4 3 2 1

LIBRARY OF CONGRESS CATALOGING IN PUBLICATION DATA

DePree, Gordon.
  Faces of God.

  1. Meditations. I. DePree, Gladis, 1933–   joint
author. II. Title.
BV4832.2.D45 1980   242   80-14384
ISBN 0-664-24350-9

Preface

In the past few years a restlessness has taken hold of many of us. We have felt a hunger to reach out beyond the old bounds of denominationalism and doctrine, a longing to know what it is that binds us not only to those whose faith is expressed like ours, but to all men. Out of this restlessness new words have grown, which have deep significance.

These words, *Faces of God*, present a whole new life concept. They have made it possible for us to discover a deep melding of the sacred and secular —in fact, they have made all of life so filled with the presence of God that there is no ungodly place. They make it possible to look into the face of every person and see there the wonder of life, the greatest miracle.

Try these words yourself, today. Look into the face of every person you meet with a consciousness that he or she is a face of God. You may be amazed at the things that happen!

GORDON AND GLADIS DEPREE

Themes

Suddenly one day
It happened.
>I stood there in the crowd
>Cursing its density and anonymity,
>Angry that my feet had been stepped on
>And no one stopped to ask my pardon . . .

Then it hit me.
>I felt the life flowing out of me
>Into the bodies around me,
>And their life flowing into mine.
>>I looked into faces for the first time,
>>Realizing that I was not only myself,
>>But I was a part of them as well.
>>They and I were expressions of the same force—
>>Life,
>>Coming from somewhere,
>>Housed in these bodies,
>>Looking out of these eyes . . .

>>>And then I recognized them—
>>>These were the faces of God!

1

Sometimes it all seems so impossible
That these people pushing past me in the shopping mall,
These endless forms
Parading through the hamburger shop,
Are the faces of God.
    God, I used to think of you as an old man,
    Sitting in heaven or somewhere,
        I never thought of you as young and old,
        As man and woman,
        As child and aged . . .
            This takes a little while
            To get used to.
            You have so many faces,
            And each one so different
            That it almost throws me back
            To my original quandary
            Of what you really look like.

But there is a difference, now . . .
I don't have to get away from the crowd
To find out.

*R*ecognizing the stranger
As a face of God
Takes so much of the suspicion and hostility
Out of life.

Perhaps I have never met you before . . .
But if I look at you with an open face,
Accepting you as a valid person,
With no need to judge
Whether you conform to my standards or not,
Will you really seem to be a stranger?
Or will we have the vague feeling
That we must have met somewhere before?

Somehow viewing the stranger as a face of God
Changes him as well as me.
For if I have seen God in him,
How can he see less in himself?

*A*n invisible God
Is a very handy kind to have.
        I can't see him,
        And hopefully, the arrangement is mutual.
          It is like a small child
          Covering his face with his fingers
          And calling slyly,
          "You can't see me!"

But when that invisible God
Shines out of the eyes
Of the faces I meet every day,
     There is no game of hide-and-seek.
        We are here,
        You see me and I see you.
        The game is over,
           And a new awareness is upon us.
           There is no room for tricks now,
           Or little games of deceit.

And always about life there is this air of resolution,
Of things having been previously decided.
For I am as one
Who has seen the invisible God
In your face.

Be subject to one another out of reverence. . . .

—Ephesians 5:21 NEB

$\mathcal{I}$n knowing and loving you
Deeply
I have become a part of the groundspring of love
Which is God.

Sometimes I realize
I have looked at you so often
I hardly see you.
You are more a feeling than a face,
   A feeling of what you mean to me,
   What you share with me,
   What you do for me . . .
         But I must remember you have your own face,
         Are your own person.

And to that person I owe
All the gentleness and respect and sense of wonder
I owe God.
For you are God come closer to me
Than in any other face.

*T*hey get up in the morning,
Tousled and sleepy-eyed,
>Scrambling for the bathroom,
>Reading the back of cereal boxes,
>Communicating in monosyllables.

And then I look at them in the morning light
As though I had never seen them before.
>Our children,
>Young forms of life
>Come from somewhere mysterious,
>Channeled through our bodies,
>>Yet original persons.
>Children, who yesterday were only dreams.
These are the faces of God.

God,
I owe them as much respect as they owe me.

"So if you are about to offer your gift to God at the altar and there you remember that your brother has something against you, leave your gift there in front of the altar and go at once to make peace with your brother. . . ."

—Matthew 5:23 TEV

*W*hen I think of myself
And you
As faces of God,
Praying seems different . . .
 Should I still close my eyes
 And pray to somewhere,
  Or should we open our eyes
  And look at each other,
  Aware of our mutual life
   And the source of life beyond us both?

What would happen if we prayed about a problem,
Looking at each other?
If we prayed about a worry,
Looking at each other?
If we prayed about an anger,
Looking at each other?

It is not as though we pray to each other,
But how could I look into your face,
A face of God,
And be a hypocrite?

And it repented the Lord that he had made man on the earth, and it grieved him at his heart.

—Genesis 6:6 KJV

C reativity,
That restless, turning, twisting force,
Is always at work in me.

In the process of creating,
I will make mistakes.
I will hurt others,
    And bring pain to myself.
But when I reach those low points,
Let me remember that everything creative and alive
Has flaws.
    Flaws are almost the mark of our authenticity,
    Our handcraftedness.

In the Genesis story
Even God had second thoughts,
Regrets,
About this imperfect creature he had put on the earth.
But he went on creating . . .

    Where else is there to go?

8

. . . God, who is not partial and takes no bribe.

—Deuteronomy 10:17 RSV

The world of our awareness
Has become more complex.
>We can no longer march off
>To squelch social uprisings,
>Singing *A Mighty Fortress is our God,*
>>For the other side may rise up and ask
>>Whose God?
>>Is he not our God as well?

If God is in our wars,
He is on both sides,
>Staring from the eyes of hungry children,
>Clutching in the hands of grief-torn women,
>Beating in the hearts of young men loath to die,
>>Bleeding when we bleed,
>>Weeping for our blindness and stupidity
>>And our inhumanity to one another . . .
>>>To ourselves,
>>>For we are all one.

I believe in one God.

And the Lord God formed man of the dust of the ground. . . .

—Genesis 2:7 KJV

A nameless longing
Can come over me while walking down a country road,
A calling out in words I do not know
In answer to voices that I cannot hear.
    Some wordless whisper reaches out of me
    To ask secrets of the trees along the road,
    To ask them how bark and leaf
    Are related to skin and bone,
        And how the change was made,
        Or if the tie ever existed
        Between sap and blood.

        And even stones,
        Ungrowing, unmoving chemical chunks . . .
        They seem to call to me,
        To invite my hands to touch,
        To establish some long-lost relationship,
        Some kinship.

        And the road and the sky,
        They call to me . . .
Is it so strange?
I am made of the stuff of the earth,
And life calls to life.

And the Lord God . . . breathed into his nostrils the breath of life. . . .

—Genesis 2:7 KJV

*T*he universal
Must become personal
To be understood.
　　　And I must stand alone
　　　In the quiet
　　　To experience what it means
　　　That I am a face of God.

I caught it in the crowd,
That blazing fire of life shining from eyes,
　　　And now I feel it beating in my private heart,
　　　Rushing in my lungs,
　　　Coursing through my veins . . .
　　　　　This gift of life,
　　　　　Which is God.
　　　　　　　And I stand still,
　　　　　　　Listening to the pounding of my heart,
　　　　　　　Knowing that I am an act of God,
　　　　　　　A miracle.

Miracles are past?
How could they be . . .
I am very present.

*W*hen I think of life as a gift of God,
A miracle,
>It is as much an affront to say
>I believe in God but not in myself,
>As to say
>I believe in myself but not in God.

Which person is the atheist?

>To disbelieve in God
>Is to doubt
>The origin and source of all life,
>>But to disbelieve in myself
>>Is to downgrade and negate
>>The creative force that lives uniquely
>>In me.
>>It is a personal affront . . .

If I have the courage to believe in myself
And others
As faces of God,
I will have the courage to believe anything.

For if ye forgive men their trespasses, your heavenly Father will also forgive you.
—Matthew 6:14 KJV

*W*hen I look at the persons around me
And see each one as a face of God,
How do I view the old word
Sin?
Is it still something I do against God?

God, this gets uncomfortable
If you've moved in next door,
Or sit across the breakfast table in the morning.
        I can't even use the old
        Sin-and-forgiveness machinery,
        Where I slog along all week
        And get forgiven on the weekend.
                Now, when something happens,
                I can't stare at you with a wooden face for six days,
                And wait for Sunday.

Come to think of it,
Trespass is a very earthy word.
I've never been in danger of trespassing
The gates of heaven.
        But I have seen
        NO TRESPASSING
        Posted on my neighbor's property.

"The kingdom of God is like a man who scatters seed in his field. He sleeps at night, . . . and all the while the seeds are sprouting and growing. Yet he does not know how it happens. . . .

—Mark 4:26, 27 TEV

I can call myself a sower of seeds,
The parent of a child,
The originator of an idea,
The composer of a song.
> But there is always about creation
> The vague feeling that I am not the original impulse,
> That there is an impulse beyond me,
> That I am only the conduit
> Through which the greater power operates.
While I sleep and wake,
The seeds are sprouting and growing,
And I never fully know how it happens . . .
> That is the wonder,
> The miracle of Life.

14

But if any provide not for his own, and specially for those of his own house, he hath denied the faith, and is worse than an infidel.

—1 Timothy 5:8 KJV

*F*idelity
Is a very human word
For trust and responsibility
And the keeping of promises.

> Infidelity
> Is also a very human word,
> Encountered almost everywhere in our world
> As breach of trust,
> Shirking of responsibility,
> And the breaking of promises.

> > But how can it be said
> > That one who does not keep his human promises
> > Is worse than an infidel?

Because once we have become aware
Of the holy nature of our relationships,
> To turn away from those relationships
> Is not only to turn away from persons.
> It is to turn away
> From a very personal
> Face of God.

I thank him who has made me equal to the task, Christ Jesus our Lord. . . .

—1 Timothy 1:12 NEB

*T*o dream of what the world can be,
Of what you and I can be as persons,
Is easy.

To implement those dreams
We need direction,
A strong creative direction
That can overcome the destructive element
So real in all of us.

*. . . and that is what being a Christian
Means to me at this point . . .*
     To follow a person
     Who made our collective dream of what man can be
     A reality.

Discipline, no doubt, is never pleasant; at the time it seems painful, but in the end it yields for those who have been trained by it the peaceful harvest of an honest life.

—Hebrews 12:11 NEB

*T*hat drag in me,
Always pulling me down,
Or to one side . . .
        Yet there stands that center core,
        Ready to snap back
        And get me in the flow of things.
                It is almost like an inner exercise,
                The flexing of muscles I cannot see,
                Yet which are the binders of my whole being.

The temptation comes to despise someone for a fool—
        Then I think of him as a face of God.
The temptation comes to lord it over someone—
        Then I think of her as a face of God.
The temptation comes to envy someone's power and position—
        Then I think of her as a face of God.
The temptation comes to look down on someone poor, or uneducated—
        Then I think of him as a face of God.

Is God a fool, or someone to be manipulated?
Is he someone I should envy, or look down on?
        When I ask the questions,
        I do not even have to answer them,
        But feel myself pulled toward center again
        And again
        And again . . .

17

. . . let every one speak the truth with his neighbor, for we are members one of another.

—Ephesians 4:25 RSV

*W*hen I speak the truth,
My face is turned toward you.
        I have nothing to hide.
                I can look at you openly.
                My words need not be guarded.

                But one little deal,
                Here and there,
                        Under the table
                        And not quite aboveboard,
                And my eyes begin to take on a less
                Direct look.
                Because I dare not look at you directly,
                You have the feeling that the world
                Is a crooked place.
                        And avert your eyes,
                                For fear someone will take advantage of you.

Please look at me,
And let me look at you,
        Or in guarding our possessions
        We have all lost our most valuable treasure:
        An honest-to-God face.

He has made known to us his hidden purpose . . . that the universe, all in
heaven and on earth, might be brought into a unity in Christ.

—Ephesians 1:9, 10 NEB

*R*eligious beliefs
Are notorious dividers of people.
> And it is a problem . . .
> How can I be loyal to my own beliefs
> And still be accepting of others.
> > I mean, really care about my faith
> > And truly accept others who believe differently?

This thing Jesus Christ lived
And died
To bring to the world
Is so enormous, so deep and true and all-encompassing,
That if I could understand and implement
one-tenth of it,
> I could accept, in a heart bubbling over with
> Love and largeness,
> Every person in my world,
> Whether he accepted me or not.

And when I accept you
Just as you are,
It's rather difficult for you to turn around
And reject me.

How convenient it is
To accord to Jesus Christ the honor of being
The son of God,
Forgetting that we too share this honor,
With all the electrifying responsibility and potential
This infers.

> You are the Christ, the son of the living God,
> Peter said,
> And not long after, he denied that he ever knew him.
> > *You be God's son, Jesus,*
> > *You hang there on the cross, and bleed for the*
> > *Sins of the world.*
> > *I'll worship you and say Our Fathers,*
> > *But don't get me mixed up in this sonship affair.*
> > > *Me, a son of God?*
> > > *No thanks. From what I can see*
> > > *It costs too much.*

We are the sons and daughters of the living God.
And only in knowing it and acknowledging it,
In all its frightening and exciting dimensions,
Will life take on its deepest meaning.

". . . he . . . ate the bread offered to God."

—Mark 2:26 TEV

$\mathcal{I}$n viewing persons as the faces of God,
What I give to God and what I do for my brother
Seem to melt into one.
     It also puts me in the right position as a giver.
     When I give to God, I must give upward.
     When I give to people, I tend to give downward.
     Perhaps the median between the two
     Is simply straightforward.

When my brother eats the bread offered to God,
It should not seem strange.
Whom do I expect to eat it . . .
God?
Only if he has many mouths.

. . . following the course of this world, . . . the spirit that is now at work in the sons of disobedience.

—Ephesians 2:2 RSV

$\mathcal{W}$hen I look around,
How can I possibly accept everybody,
    Just everybody,
    As a face of God?

      This one lies, and that one cheats,
      That fellow was involved in a scandal,
      This one screams at his wife,
         This boy is on drugs,
         And this girl is promiscuous,
         That woman manipulates her family,
         And the whole neighborhood.
      Is it not an insult to God
      To call these his faces?

My face can become distorted.
Pushed into shape or out of shape
By *"what's done"*
By lack of awareness of who I am . . .

      But is a dirty face
      Any less a face?

. . . and [Joseph] fled and got out of the house.

—Genesis 39:12 RSV

S aying yes to life
Is a good idea,
Until I come upon a situation that requires a no.
　　Yes-yes-yes
　　May become no more than weakness,
　　Letting life trample me
　　Instead of flowing through me.

The word no
Can be as creative as the word yes.
The difference between a creative no
And a negative no
Is the impulse it stems from.
　　When no can be said as a declaration of freedom,
　　It can be a sound of joy—
　　　　And leave one with the inner glow
　　　　That he has said
　　　　Yes
　　　　To something larger.

The wicked flee when no one pursues, but the righteous are bold as a lion.

—Proverbs 28:1 RSV

*F*lee . . .
To run in terror
From some real or imagined danger—
This is never an act of faith,
But of fear.

> When I am running
> From something,
> I am not going anywhere.
> I am in retreat,
> Regressing,
> Reducing my grasp on life.

Only when I am running
Toward some goal, some objective,
Are my motions the actions of faith.

The steps are the same.
> But what a difference
> In running from
> And running toward.

. . . God did not lead them by way of the land, . . . although that was near. . . .
But God led the people round by the way of the wilderness. . . .

—Exodus 13:17, 18 RSV

During one lifetime
The evolution of man's awareness seems slow.
 We do a dance,
 With one step forward
 And two steps backward,
   And only live up to half of what we know
   Most of the time.

   Why? Why must we go through this agonizing process?
   Why are we not born perfect,
   Knowing all that is our birthright,
   Living in full awareness of our potential,
   Shining containers of the life of God?

The recorded history of man has been a constant struggle.
Is it possible that awareness
Comes only through conflict?
 And the sum of our personal awarenesses
 Becomes collective?

We no longer hang children
For stealing a loaf of bread . . .
 Not in public,
 At least.

We all reflect as in a mirror the splendour of the Lord; thus we are transfigured into his likeness, from splendour to splendour. . . .

—2 Corinthians 3:18 NEB

This morning I looked in the mirror
And thought of myself as a face of God.
I felt both elated
And deflated.

    I felt elated because I belong,
    Am a part of a larger body of life,
    Because my life is not restricted to this one body,
    But is a part of all that lives . . .
        And although I have only this once to live,
        Yet I was, before I had this face,
        And will be, as long as there is life,
        As long as there is God.

I felt deflated
Because as an individual I am essentially isolated,
Alone, powerless,

    No matter how many times I look in the mirror,
    Or think my own thoughts, or claim to be my own person,
    I in essence am a stranger to myself,
        Almost as much a stranger as I am to others,
        Always discovering, never knowing fully.

I felt elated and deflated, two forces in one emotion.
Like sugar and salt
In the same cup of coffee.

26

"Know therefore, that the Lord your God is not giving you this good land to possess because of your righteousness; for you are a stubborn people."

—Deuteronomy 9:6 RSV

Sometimes we thank God
For our blessings,
    Thinking ever so privately
    We must deserve them somehow,
    Or they would never have come to us.

        But anyone who has recognized God
        In the faces of flood victims,
        Or seen him in the eyes of children
        Torn apart in war,
            Or glimpsed him in the bony frames of famine,
            Or wondered at the destruction of tidal wave
            And earthquake,
            Where the good and evil alike
            Are swept to their graves . . .
                Finds the cosmic system
                Of punishment and reward
                    A little harder to understand.

I don't pretend to understand it.
But I do hope I know better
Than to get conceited when something good comes
To me.

It is easy
To get sucked into the vacuum
Of owning things,
     And end up finding out that they own you.

How hard it is to strike a balance
Between what I need and what I want!
     The list of needs grows:
     A house, a car,
     A better house, two cars,
     A summer house, two better cars,
    On and on it goes, until I find my body chasing
    Things
    Which have nothing to do with my real self.

But what does life mean?
What do I want?
Where did the time go to think about ideas,
To waste hours deliciously with a friend,
To put a kite together with a child?

Jesus Christ,
How could you have been so right
Two thousand years ago?

Fools make a mock at sin: but among the righteous there is favour.

—Proverbs 14:9 KJV

*W*hen I have a consciousness
Of every person as a face of God,
What is a dirty joke?
>It may be a sex joke,
>But it will not be the sex that makes it dirty.

>>Any joke
>>That makes a person feel small,
>>That puts someone down,
>>Or belittles him because
>>Of his race or social standing,
>>>Any joke that laughs at human hurt,
>>>Or winks at brokenness
>>>Or wrong relationships
>>>>As being the funniest thing out,
>>>>>Is dirty.
>>>>>It is dirty
>>>>>Because hurting another person
>>>>>Is not funny.
>>>>>Hurt is dirt.

*F*or many years
We have had the mistaken notion
That all the problems of the world
Can be solved with a dollar bill.

    In Jesus' time
    The Pharisees came to ask him if they should
    Pay taxes,
    And Jesus, looking at a silver coin,
    Asked whose face and name were engraved on it.
        "The Emperor's," they said.
        "Well then, pay to the Emperor what is his," Jesus replied.

Has God's face
Ever been on a coin?
    We are the coin
    That bears the living likeness of God.
    Giving of ourselves
        With whatever that may include,
        Is the only legal currency
        Of the kingdom of heaven.

Jesus took the blind man by the hand and led him. . . .

—Mark 8:23 TEV

$\mathcal{I}$t all sounds so great in theory . . .
　　　To identify with the pain of man,
　　　To participate in man's brokenness.

But in real life
Do I have the nerve that Jesus Christ had
　　　To take the blind man by the hand
　　　And walk through the village with him,
　　　　　To sit with the alcoholic
　　　　　And see him through a tough night,
　　　　　　　To associate with a family
　　　　　　　Going through divorce,
　　　　　　　Unafraid
That I will be thought to have the wrong kind of friends?

What kind of friends are the wrong kind?
Does not the weakness or strength
Lie in me?

But when you pray, go into a room by yourself, shut the door, and pray to your Father who is there in the secret place. . . .

—Matthew 6:6 NEB

*J*esus Christ disliked showy prayers.
They turned him off.
>Loud prayers,
>Long prayers,
>Prayers telling God what he has been doing
>Ever since the dawn of history,
>>Prayers describing heaven and hell
>>For God,
>>And what he should do about the world situation,
>>All couched in words that no sensible person
>>Would use in a face-to-face encounter.

Sometimes quiet words will do.
Sometimes even words are superfluous,
And can block the pure flow of wordless communication
With the infinite . . .
>>That warm glow
>>Or sharp pain,
>>That surge of joy . . .
>>These are almost too abstract to be spoken,
Too sacred to share,
Unless I trust you very much.

If the Spirit is the source of our life, let the Spirit also direct our course.

—Galatians 5:25 NEB

𝒥t is at times difficult to understand
Why
If the Spirit of God is the source of our life,
Lives can get so mixed up,
So off course.

    But since the beginning of time
    The gift of life
    Has never been an unqualified good.
    Our senses, which serve us impartially and well,
    Bring us a fragrance one moment
    And a stench the next.

Yet it is always there . . .
    The inner voice,
    The feeling for right,
    The unquenchable longing of man to be free
    Even from his self-imposed prisons . . .
The spirit of God
Through all the maze of life,
Directing our course.

33

*W*hat would happen
If we set aside one day a week
And called it
Observation day?
     Suppose for one day we would awaken with a sense
     Of life as a miracle.
          We would watch the sun rise with a sense of awe,
          Or listen to the rain strike the roof,
          And feel the wonder of the rhythms of the universe.
     Suppose we actually looked at each other,
     And saw the beauty of the life force in each other,
     Coordinating limb and eye
     With that indefinable something called personality . . .

     What if we really looked and saw and felt
     Consciously,
     Once a week?
     What would it do for our ability to worship?

34

". . . although no man is with us, remember, God is witness between you and me."

—Genesis 31:50 RSV

*N*o agreement
Or act
Between two persons
Ever goes unwitnessed.
        God is there.
                And whether that fact brings fear
                Or joy
                Depends on the two persons involved.

                Do I welcome the fact that you are a face of God?
                Does it make my promises to you
                Take on a sacred quality,
                And every relationship between us
                A celebration of life, face to face . . .
                        Or does the fact of who you are
                        Bring judgment on me
                        For having desecrated that which is holy
                        And belittled that which is infinite?

No interchange between two persons
Ever goes unwitnessed.
They are their own witnesses . . .
                And they are the faces of God.

. . . and he would have liked to remain unrecognized, but this was impossible.

—Mark 7:24 NEB

$\mathcal{I}$n our world
Many of us seek some kind of recognition.
We struggle to build ourselves up in some field,
We work to be recognized.
It is hard to come by.

     But here was this Jesus,
     Trying not to be recognized,
     And finding that he could not hide.
     What was there about him
     That made it impossible for him to melt
     Into the anonymous crowd?

Could it have been that shining clear awareness
Of who he was,
     Who God was,
     What life was,
     That made him stand out,
     Unable to be hidden?

"Remember this! Whoever does not receive the Kingdom of God like a child will never enter it."

—Mark 10:15 TEV

*T*o children
The world is fresh and new.
They have no preconceived ideas,
Nor points to prove.
> Things are the way they seem,
> Yet there is room to imagine
> That anything could happen.

Things are simple,
And life is food,
> Clothing and shelter,
> Generously laced with love.

And only those who retain
The free imagination of children
> Could imagine such a thing
> As that God is king
> Of this mixed-up world.

Who else could believe it?

Surely you know that you are God's temple, where the Spirit of God dwells. . . .
the temple of God is holy; and that temple you are.

—1 Corinthians 3:16, 17 NEB

*S*exual morality
Is not a thing in itself.
It is a part of a whole moral code
Which says I must love and respect
Myself
And all the selves around me so much
That I will do nothing to hurt or destroy
Sexually
Or otherwise.

Sexuality
Is the most directly creative force
We have been given.
When it is used to create,
It is right,
When it is used to destroy,
It is wrong . . .
Even within legal bounds.

Be kindly affectioned one to another with brotherly love; in honour preferring one another.

—Romans 12:10 KJV

$\mathcal{J}$n a world of tigers,
Who can afford to be
Kindly?
> Yet the very word *kindly*
> Has a warm glow around it
> And draws one like an open fireplace,
> Pulling at longings almost made obsolete
> By technology.

Kindly is not only a description of a person,
It is a description of all this person does.
> When he shares, he does so kindly.
> When he warns, he does so kindly.
> When he agrees,
> And even when he disagrees,
> It is kindly.

At the risk of being considered obsolete,
Kindly
Is a way of living and relating
That I would like to cultivate.

*W*e build up
Polite cultural defenses
Against honesty.
> The open face,
> The unadorned truth,
> The frank comment,
> The unambiguous statement
> We seem to leave behind with childhood.
>> And as we grow,
>> We accumulate a thousand tricks and artifices
>> To divert and disguise
>> Our every thought.

Then someone is very honest with us,
And it is shocking.
We almost consider
The naked truth
Obscene.

$\mathcal{T}$rying to accept people
Is like trying to fly without wings,
Until one has found a basic life concept
Big enough to make acceptance automatic.

I used to stare at saffron yellow robes,
        Afro hairdos and clerical collars,
        Clenched militant fists and dreary pietists,
        And pictures of Mao,
                And try graciously to accept them.

Then the scene changed,
And eyes were all I saw, each with a life-light shining
Like a candle,
Each trying desperately to fight the primal darkness,
To say *Let there be light* in his own way.
        And when the faces came back into focus,
        Each one was delightful.

Accept?
Who am I to limit the expressions on God's face?

"You know that the men who are considered rulers have power over the people. . . . This, however, is not the way it is among you. If one of you wants to be great, he must be the servant of the rest. . . ."

—Mark 10:42, 43 TEV

*T*hat is not the way it is among you,
You who have seen God in the faces of men.
> When you are in a position of authority,
> You do not take it as an opportunity
> For self-aggrandizment,
> You do not lord it over your underlings,
> And rob their self-respect and creativity,
> You do not take the credit for everything,
> And leave the work and the blame for others.
>> That is not the way it is for you . . .

More is expected of you,
Because you have understood
> That a position of authority
> Is an opportunity to develop the best
> In others,
> That it is a life situation in which to
> Identify deeply with co-workers,
> A framework in which to develop
> The self-respect and creativity of others,
> A situation in which the leader
> Shares the credit,
> And absorbs the blame.

That is how it is to be among you.

42

When he came ashore, he saw a great crowd; and his heart went out to them,
because they were like sheep without a shepherd; and he had much to teach
them.

—Mark 6:34 NEB

*L*ike sheep without a shepherd . . .
How better could our world be described today!
     Masses and millions
     Living with no awareness
     Of our connectedness to each other,
        Caught in brambles,
        Lost,
        And munching what scraggy grass we can find.

These people gathered around Jesus
Awoke in him an almost overwhelming sense
Of the greatness of his work.
     Here they were,
     Sons and daughters of God
     Who had never been awakened to an awareness
     Of their potential,
     Or to the miracle of their lives—
        And if he did not teach them,
        Who would?

And if I do not,
Who will?

*Then Pharisees and scribes came to Jesus from Jerusalem and said, "Why do
your disciples transgress the tradition of the elders?" . . .He answered them . . .
"for the sake of your tradition, you have made void the word of God."*

—Matthew 15:1, 6 RSV

*T*here is nothing that will make one scuttle for cover
Under tradition
So fast
As trying to help children grow up.
    I can explore,
    Explode,
    Discard this idea for that,
    But what do I teach my children?

        I could revert,
        And teach them about the God out there,
        And build in them fear and guilt.
            It might work for a while . . .
        But if they were strong enough
        To outgrow the fears and guilts,
            What would happen to their belief in God?

No.
I will not take refuge under tradition.
I am still a child in this universe,
And as such, I will explore with my children
The mysteries of life.

44

*A*ctually,
Only persons of great faith
Can afford to doubt.

If I have a great sustaining faith
That God is,
That he is the point of origin of all life,
    I can afford to doubt the forms,
    Institutions,
    Dogmas,
    And rituals of that faith as being final
        And still have a deep and vibrant faith.

There is positive doubt,
And positive doubt might be defined
As the questioning of a smaller idea
In order to believe in a larger one.
    Or perhaps it comes in the reverse order—
    Having glimpsed some magnificent overpowering truth
    Makes me doubt the finality of anything less.

*L*ight,
New ideas,
New trends, inspiring thoughts,
      Creative worship, speaking in tongues,
      Encounter groups, communes,
      Seeing God in the faces of men . . .
All of these bombard our senses,
Sometimes leaving us confused
As to where the past went
And where the future is going.

      What is good,
      And good for what?
Finding a light is only half the battle.
Learning to use it is the other half.
      A lighted lamp put under a bowl will go out.
      Under a bed, it could cause a fire.
      Only when put where it can shed light is it good.

Light is a fire,
And can burn or bless.

S omewhere along the line
We have picked up a deep misunderstanding of the word
Self.
>   We mistake our grossness and superficiality
>   For self,
>   When actually it is in the pursuit of superficialities
>   That we smother self,
>   Our God-self,
>   That deep cry of the genuine life within.

If I can be aware of the worth of my life,
The God-life within me,
>   I will not be content to eat the husks of meaning
>   In an alienated pig-field of despair.
And knowing that my selfhood
Is the most cherished thing I possess,
I will not squander it
Endlessly.

Each man should examine his own conduct for himself; then he can measure his achievement by comparing himself with himself and not with anyone else.

—Galatians 6:4–5 NEB

*M*ost of us
Have some kind of self-image,
    And buried even deeper than our practical
    Self-image,
    There is a list of longings
    Of what we would like to be,
    Or feel we could have been if—

Maybe it's not practical.
Maybe nobody does it, and it's never been heard of.
    But how does my outer self as I live my life
    Measure against my inner self
    As I know my self?
        Am I ignoring the secret glow inside me?
        Am I letting my dreams slip,
        Or living not quite the way I want to live?

I can't measure myself
Against the success or failure of others.
There's not another face of God
Just like mine.

Sometimes I sit in a worship service
And hear these words.
And they seem like an echo from man's distant past,
From the days before we knew
That we were the faces of God,
> That he could no more leave us
> Than our life could leave us,
>> And even then,
>> We would be in his presence.

No,
I'm not afraid that God will go away,
Or kick me out . . .
> The only thing that plagues me
> As I sit listening to these old words
> Is my own sleepiness,
> My own lack of awareness,
> My own insensitivity to the wonder of this gift
> Of life,
> Which is mine
> Whether I use it or not.

*This is how one should regard us, as servants of Christ and stewards of the
mysteries of God.*

—1 Corinthians 4:1 RSV

God,
How few of us want to be considered servants!
We don't mind wearing the uniform,
And keeping the brass buttons shined,
> But when it comes to carrying out
> The dirty dishes,
> Why should I do it?

There is a basic formula
Which can tie us strongly to life . . .
The stimulus of work perceived,
And the response of doing it
Automatically,
Without the question of our smallness or greatness,
But because it needs to be done.

> Be your servant?
> Why should I?
> > Because it ties me to you,
> > And that's what life is all about.

My brothers, believing as you do in our Lord Jesus Christ, . . . you must never show snobbery.

—James 2:1 NEB

$\mathcal{T}$he should
Of the person who follows Jesus Christ
Goes very deep.

It is not a childlike should,
Taught by punishment and reward
And obeyed for the same reasons,
But a mature should,
A reason why or why not
That reaches from the center of my consciousness
To the farthest echoes of my imagination.

Someone has shown me what can be,
And I have sensed the essence of his way . . .
A gentle, plain man,
Who needed no ostentation to prove
The worth of his life.
And believing in him as I do,
How could I ever participate
In something like snobbery?
In fact,
Why should I?

Wherever he went, . . . all who touched him were cured.

—Mark 6:56 NEB

*P*eople are sick in many ways,
    Sick with fear and pride,
    Sick with prejudice,
    With shoddy illusions of the real values in life . . .
        Sick with despair or boredom,
        Broken from a lack of meaning,
        Or any sense of cohesiveness or purpose in life.

When I,
As one aware that these are the faces of God,
Walk about,
What difference do I make?
When my life touches the lives of those around me,
Do I bring any kind of awareness
Or healing?
        Or am I overcome with the whole terrible scene,
        And concede that these could not possibly be
        The faces of God?

And there appeared to them tongues like flames of fire, . . . resting on each one.

—Acts 2:3 NEB

*T*he Spirit of God
Is a great binding force,
Shared by many,
Making the many one.
  Yet the picture
  Of a tongue of flame on each head
  Is significant.
    Peter, plus the Spirit of God,
    Became one kind of man.
      John, plus the Spirit of God,
      Became another kind of man.

Each man of the group
Became aware of his intense identification with
The group,
And at the same time, of his own unique worth
As an individual.

Do we have this same spirit
When we worship together today?

*J*esus Christ
Was born into a world
Of do not touch, do not taste, do not handle.
He was taught to leave the leper to his fate,
That the rules had been made
For the protection of the majority,
At the cost of the person.

But somehow
He could not forget the leper
With his torn clothes and matted hair,
Cast outside the city to die.
The rules were there,
But they were not enough . . .
And defying his tradition,
He touched the lepers
And they were healed.
How?
I don't know.
But if I ever had the courage to break the rules
And sacrifice my own safety
For the sake of one life, the way he did,
I might find out.

54

Thus it is the men of faith who share the blessing with faithful Abraham.

—Galatians 3:9 NEB

E ver since men have had the idea
Of one God,
There have been two kinds of worshipers:
    The great believers,
    And the frightened followers.

The great believers,
Or men of faith,
Had a feeling about God,
    A feeling that went on,
    No matter how the rules and regulations
    Were changed.

    Then there were the frightened followers
    Who were all confused
    Every time the rules were changed,
        Because they did not have the
        Great feeling about God.

Which one am I?

For everything that God created is good, and nothing is to be rejected when it is taken with thanksgiving. . . .

—1 Timothy 4:4 NEB

*W*ith this idea in mind
I can walk down the dirtiest, most squalid
Section of town
And find God there.
>God asleep drunk on the sidewalk,
>In a face that was created for awareness and consciousness,
>A face that rejected the responsibility
>Of consciousness and awareness
>And decided to forget it all.

Behind the manicured lawns
On the other end of town
There are people making the same choice,
>And in the pews on Sunday morning
>Others choose to reject the responsibility
>Of consciousness and awareness
>By mumbling pious phrases,
>And hoping they will get them to heaven.

Church, wine, manicured lawns . . .
Everything that God created is good,
>But only if it sharpens my thankfulness for life
>And adds to my awareness of the greatness of that gift,
>Is it good for me.

"Did I not tell your messengers whom you sent to me . . . 'what the Lord speaks, that will I speak'?"

—Numbers 24:12,13 RSV

$\mathcal{F}$ew of us would have the audacity
To claim that the words we speak
Are the words of God.
     Even in the Old Testament passage
     The sentence ends in a question mark,
     Which is about where I end
     When I think about it.

     But if I am a face of God,
     Must I not also be a mouth of God,
          Speaking what he cannot speak,
          Except through me,
          Encouraging where he cannot encourage,
          Except through me,
               Exploring and exchanging ideas
               Where he is silent, except through me?

Yet it is a startling thought.
     If I were aware for one day
     That God speaks when I speak,
          It would either temper the tone of my tongue
          Or broaden my image
          Of the range of God's emotions.

In reaching for wholeness
As a person
A whole new range of creative thought
Is possible.

Prayer can be so many things
I never dreamed of.
It can contain shocking, almost irreverent,
Or what I used to consider irreverent,
Phrases.

Sometimes I can't tell if I'm praying
Or swearing,
Like,

God, that man is beautiful!
Thank you for making such a restless,
Hungry, insatiably curious
Form of your face for me to know.

Praying or swearing?
I can't tell that much difference anymore,
Unless I'm saying it in vain.

Restore unto me the joy of thy salvation; and uphold me with thy free spirit.

—Psalm 51:12 KJV

God,
I need some outside help tonight.
I want so much to be free,
But I don't feel free.

> I know it all in my head . . .
> That your life is living in me,
> That my life is a miracle,
> > But in my heart
> > It seems as if life is pressing in on me
> > And squeezing me,
> > Until I feel empty and limp.

Free . . .
What can that word mean
When my life belongs to so many other people,
When I get squeezed between the generation gap
And the tax bill,
And I want to walk out of the door and keep on walking
and never stop . . .
Then what does it mean to be free?
God,
I need some help outside myself tonight . . .
Or are you really inside me?

At this they were completely dumbfounded, for they had not understood the incident of the loaves; their minds were closed.

*W*hat a robber a closed mind can be!
Because we do not want to accept things,
In our minds they have never happened,
   And because they have never happened,
   They cannot happen now.
      They can never happen in the future
      Because we did not hear or see them in the past . . .

And on we go
Through life's experiences,
Never knowing God's power
Or our own potential,
Because our minds are shut like window shades.

If just for today my mind could be open,
What would I see?

God does not recognize these personal distinctions. . . .

—Galatians 2:6 NEB

$\mathcal{I}$n seeing every person as a face of God
We have a basis for great respect
For every living person.
>   But this great store of respect
>   Has a way of getting out of balance.
>   We forget to divide it evenly . . .
>>   We overly honor some, so that we make fools
>>   Of ourselves,
>>   And snub others, so that we make fools
>>   Of them.
When we learn neither to tremble before the high
Nor to scorn the personhood of the lowly,
But view all with an open face,
We are learning a sense of cosmic balance.

So God created man in his own image, . . . male and female created he them.

—Genesis 1:27 KJV

$\mathcal{I}$ am a woman face of God,
I am a part of the creative power.

    I am tenderness and warmth,
    My arms open
    And take in what needs comfort,
    My eyes open
    And take in situations intuitively,
    My body opens
    And takes in seed,
        And creates life.
        I am a woman face of God.

    Yet in me
    There is hardness and courage.
    My hands grasp work,
    And my eyes see goals.
    My body can be closed,
    And I can be a destroyer.

    I am a woman face of God
    Who can understand what it is to be a man.

So God created man in his own image . . . male and female created he them.

—Genesis 1:27 KJV

𝐼 am a man face of God,
I am a part of the creative power.

      I am strong and cool,
      My fists clenched
      To do what needs doing,
      My eyes squinted
      To appraise situations reasonably.
      My body gives
      And plants seed,
            And creates life.
            I am a man face of God.

      Yet in me
      There is tenderness and love.
      My hands caress,
      And my eyes smile.
      My body can be vulnerable,
      And I can be destroyed.

      I am a man face of God
      Who can understand what it is to be a woman.

Help one another to carry these heavy loads. . . .

—Galatians 6:2 NEB

How are you?
We ask it a dozen times a day—
      But how many of us really care to know?

If I ask someone, How are you?
And the answer begins to sound like
Bloody but unbowed,
      Do I edge for the door,
      Or yawn over the phone,
      Or glance at my watch,
      Mindful of the next real or imagined duty?

Sometimes my brother's troubles are too heavy to bear
On top of my own.
And why are my own so heavy?
Perhaps with sharing,
The load would get lighter
For everyone.

"*W*ho are my brothers?"
This is the basic question
On which all life concepts have rocked.
We can afford to accept some men all of the time,
And all men some of the time.
> But it is virtually impossible for us to accept
> All men all of the time
> As our undeniable brothers,
>> Sharing in their mistakes,
>> Identifying with their short-circuited ideas,
>> Accepting their crassness and stupidity
>> As a family affair . . .

Especially as Christians,
We call God our father,
And those of like faith our brothers.

But
For goodness' sake,
Whose sons are the rest of these?

"But now I tell you: love your enemies, and pray for those who persecute you, so that you will become the sons of your Father in heaven. For he makes his sun to shine on bad and good people alike. . . ."

—Matthew 5:44, 45 TEV

$\mathcal{W}$ho is my enemy?
That fellow who every time I think of him makes
A stab of anger churn inside me . . .

> Or perhaps a twist of envy,
> Or a shrug of disgust.
> He is utterly revolting,
> And I could curse him,
> Or kill him.

What would happen if I tried looking at him
As a face of God?

> Would I find that he too is a struggling person,
> Plagued with faults,
> Pushed by his fears to defend himself by robbing
> My rights, my name, my self-esteem?
>> And why has his affront to my pride hurt so much?
>> Am I too proud?
>> Am I perfect?

It is hard to look at a man as a face of God
And consider him
The enemy.

"Listen! There was a man who went out to sow. As he scattered the seed. . . ."

—Mark 4:3 TEV

*J*esus could have used direct words
In his teachings about the nature of God.
But instead he chose to speak of seeds
And fields, of birds and stones,
Of children and life situations.
If he wanted to get his message across,
Why was he not more direct?

The answer to this question should not be stated
Too clearly,
Or we fall into our own trap.
>But could it be
>That faith, and the understanding of God,
>Is an art?
>And art is meant to send spirits soaring.
>When reduced to directness,
>It becomes propaganda,
>>And all propaganda can do
>>Is to set feet marching,
>>Usually
>>Against something.

"You are mistaken. . . . you do not know either the scriptures or the power of God."

—Mark 12:24 NEB

$\mathcal{H}$ow quickly we line up
And take sides on an issue.
     There is resurrection,
     There is no resurrection . . .

At such times
It is good to see this yes and no
Flow together to form a new element,
A new concept,
     Flipping us into a state of wonder
     We had not dreamed of,
        Neither yes nor no,
           But a reality for which
           We do not even have a word.

In the history of the Hebrew people,
Respect for the land
Was a part of religious practice.
> We have not very often equated
> Reverence for God
> With respect for the soil.
> In our divided minds
> The face of the earth has had little to do
> With the face of God.

> > But walk outside
> > And take up a handful of earth.
> > Imagine a tiny brown seed in your hand,
> > Drawing life and greenness from the soil.
> > Imagine it growing, flowering,
> > Making seeds,
> > And falling back into your hand . . .
> > > This is an act of God,
> > > A life-miracle.

> > A handful of earth
> > Is a handful of life
> > The original source of which
> > Is God.
> > Is anything disconnected?

For Jesus Christ, the Son of God, . . . is not one who is "Yes" and "No." On the contrary, he is God's "Yes"; for it is he who is the "Yes" to all of God's promises.

—2 Corinthians 1:19, 20 TEV

Jesus Christ, God or Man?

From the beginning the lines were two,
God above, and man below.
> And then they came together,
> God, in the face of a man.
>> It left us shocked and puzzled,
>> And made us ask searching questions
>> About the nature of our own being.
>>> For having once recognized God
>>> In the face of a man,
>>> Being a man has never been the same.

>>> The lines have come together,
>>> And the answer to all the questions
>>> Is the same . . .
>>>> Yes!

*T*he Spirit of God,
Present in each of his creatures,
Is the life of the Creative Power in us.
    To desecrate that spirit,
    To channel that power toward destructive purposes,
    To take what was made for wholeness and goodness
    And use it for brokenness and hurt . . .

    How could I even forgive *myself?*

. . . Cain rose up against Abel his brother, and slew him.

—Genesis 4:8 KJV

*W*hen I see myself and the selves around me
As faces of God,
How do I cope with violence?
Can one face of God turn against the other?

Nature is full of violence.
Why do parasites eat the life of trees,
And snakes eat birds' eggs?
But even if living things destroy each other,
Is not more to be expected of conscious life,
Of beings with a moral conscience?

The old story of Cain and Abel is interesting
As a key to understanding violence and seeing ourselves as God's faces.
Cain killed his brother
Because he felt rejected by God.
But did he strike at God?
No . . .
He struck
Where he must have seen the rejection.

". . . I did not come to invite virtuous people, but sinners."

—Mark 2:17 NEB

*I*nvite them to what?
What was there about Jesus Christ
That attracted the "bad" people of his day?

Perhaps it was the rediscovery,
Shining through his face as he looked at them,
Of who they really were . . .
    A gaze which looked through the blighted exterior
    And saw beneath
    A face of God,
        A painful face of God,
        Twisted and marred with greed or frustration,
        Or squandered potential,
            But still there.

And when he looked at them,
They saw themselves again
Clearly.

As a follower of Jesus Christ,
Have I ever looked that inviting?

. . . what shall a man give in exchange for his soul?

—Mark 8:37 KJV

How much is a person worth?
In our savage days,
When slaves were bought and sold,
Gross monetary value was put on human heads.
    But now, in our enlightened culture,
    How do we measure the worth of a man?
    How much is he worth?
        Worth a million?
        Or is he a poor devil
        Who'll never see more than $10,000 a year?
What is he worth?
    $50,000?
    $75,000?
Or if he's penniless,
Is he worthless?

What is a person worth,
A person,
Who is an expression of the life of God?

C hristianity
Has so seldom tapped the spring
Of wish power.
It has more often been identified
As a religion of grim
Will power.

But when I can catch a vision of Jesus Christ
As a living symbol
Of all the deepest and highest
And best
That I wish for myself and my world,
A new element enters into my faith.

I really wish, with all my heart,
That I had the courage to do the imaginative things
That Jesus Christ did,
That I could be as intrepid
And as careless of the results
Of naked integrity
As he was.
I *wish* to be his follower.

Sometimes we get very uptight
About how God will accomplish his purposes
In the world.
> *As it was in the beginning,*
> *Is now, and ever shall be,*
> *World without end, Amen.*
> And that's the end of it.

> And while we go plodding along
> In our religious routines,
> Grinding through our hymns
> And sleeping through our sermons,
>> The quicksilver spirit of God
>> Can fly out of the door
>> From sheer boredom,

And might even show up in the opposite
Corner of the world,
Working through channels which we consider ungodly,
To free the faces of his creatures
From ancient wrongs.

*F*or anyone who glimpses the wonder
Of being,
The mystery of living,
There will come times of wrestling,
Of seeking the most creative directions in life.

The easiest course to follow
Is to avoid the fight,
To give in . . .
But for the person who dares to face his problems
Hand to hand in honest combat,
There will come a time when he must prove
Whether he is equal to the challenge of being
A face of God
Or not.
And after the night's wrestling,
There is a difference.
That self, so much a part of one's identity,
Is gone.
And in its place there grows a new person
So much larger
He should almost have a new name.

"I am the way; I am the truth and I am the life; no one comes to the Father except by me."

—John 14:6 NEB

*W*hat ever happened
To Christian exclusiveness?
What about
No one comes to the Father except by me?

And who was this me?
Was he not a man who sat with turncoats
And prostitutes,
A man who in the cohesive context of Judaism
Illustrated the concern of connectedness
By using a foreigner,
The good Samaritan?

No one will ever be aware
Of the source of the creative spring
Without knowing what Jesus Christ taught,
But we have often accepted Jesus Christ
To the exclusion of everyone else . . .
Was this what he meant?

The wolf also shall dwell with the lamb, and the leopard shall lie down with the kid; . . . and the lion shall eat straw like the ox. . . . They shall not hurt nor destroy . . . for the earth shall be full of the knowledge of the Lord. . . .

—Isaiah 11:6–9 KJV

A system
Where living creatures
Prey on each other
Seems to set uneasily
   On the pages of our aspirations.
   In a time of perfection
   The lamb will not fear the lion
   And the lion will eat straw like the ox.

   And what will man eat?
   Will the hunting instinct die,
   And man cease to prey
      On other forms of life?
   The bullet of the hunter
   Becomes the bullet of the killer,
   And the seriousness of what is killed
   Depends on how we view other creatures.
      The enemy becomes an animal
      And the animal becomes an enemy,
      And blood is shed.

Somewhere, deep in our consciousness,
There is horror at shed blood.

*T*here is at the core of every freedom
A grain of prohibition
Which insures the existence
Of that freedom itself.

Yet we,
So mad to be free,
Can sometimes center down
On that one sand grain of prohibition
And try to cast it out . . .
Forgetting that it may be the crucial element
Which makes the whole operate
Freely.

If I am a truly free person
I will come to the conclusion someday
That there are some things
I cannot do
And be free.

Now their deeds encompass them, they are before my face.

—Hosea 7:2 RSV

$\mathcal{H}$ow did this happen to me?
Things were going so well . . .
How did I get off the track?
    I was in a brave situation, living by imagination,
    And fear made me retreat.
        When I retreated, I found it necessary
        To justify myself
        By blaming persons,
        Systems, and institutions.
            And in blaming,
            I became alienated from them
                Until I found myself sucked into a
                Downward spiral, dizzy and gasping
                For air.
                Now here I am,
                Alone.

Who did this to me?
Did God turn his face
Against me?

Be humble always and gentle, and patient too.

—Ephesians 4:2 NEB

When I think of myself
As an individual,
    The words humble,
        Gentle,
        And patient,
        Seem restrictive.
           Where will they get me?

But when I think of myself
As only one of the multi-million faces of God,
    I know that my life, although valid,
    Is no more valid than yours,
        And my actions, although full of meaning,
        Are no more meaningful than yours,
           And that if your steps are slower than mine,
           I must be patient with you,
           As I hope you will be with me.

Humble, gentle, patient?
Where will it get me?
    I don't need to get anywhere.
    I'm there—
        But I'm still learning what it means.

Saved from what?
Hell?
And what is hell?
    Yes, I know all the answers,
    But what do they mean?

When I think of each person
As an expression of the life of God,
    What is the meaning of all these theological terms
    So deeply rooted in our culture
    That they make their way into jokes, slang, and recipes?

If hell is separation from God,
And we are the faces of God,
    What does that say about our divisions,
    About despising another person?
        If heaven is the presence of God,
        And we are the faces of God,
        What does that say about the value of openness
        And truth, communication and honesty?

Knowing all the answers is knowing nothing.
What
On earth
Do they mean?

I'm having trouble this morning,
Making a connection between
The faces of God
And a terrible crime.
> How could one who is a face of God
> Commit a mass killing?

Yesterday I saw a mother take her two-year-old,
Slam him in a chair,
And call him a brat.
> Last week I saw the despair of a boy
> Whose parents spoke of his faults in front of him
> And in front of strangers.
> > I saw the frozenness of a girl
> > Who was typed as the perfect child,
> > And would not dare to be anything less . . .
And I shuddered at the way we reject each other.

Acceptance is the creative principle,
Rejection is the destructive principle.
> And oh my God,
> How we perpetuate destruction
> From generation to generation!

And because for us there is no veil over the face, we all reflect as in a mirror the splendour of the Lord; thus we are transfigured into his likeness, from splendour to splendour. . . .

—2 Corinthians 3:18 NEB

*T*here was a time in man's awareness
When we thought we could not look on the face of God
And live.
> And we still feel it.
> If you stare at me for very long,
> We both feel uncomfortable.
>> Even an animal will look away
>> If you look into its face for more than a few seconds.

> But now there is the opposite danger.
> If we do not face each other,
> If we do not recognize our oneness,
>> We will not live.

>> Open your eyes and look at me.
>> Don't be afraid.
>> Reach out your finger and touch my hand . . .
>> Do you feel that current of life
>> Flowing from your finger to mine?

We live.
And only as we look into each other's faces,
The faces of God,
Will we know how to live.

—Mark 12:12 NEB

S ometimes we tend to dismiss popular feeling
As a cheap, sentimental,
Watered-down set of ethics.

But there is another way
Of viewing these words . . .
The feeling of the people,
People who are a collective expression
Of the life of God.

What people are feeling and needing,
Responding to and reaching for
At any given time,
Is often an indication of our deepest needs,
However twisted,
And hopes, however dim.

Popular feeling
Is something I should be attune to.

*Behold, the Lord's hand is not shortened, that it cannot save, or his ear dull,
that it cannot hear. . . .*

—Isaiah 59:1 RSV

*I*f I am a face of God,
Must I not also serve as his ears?

Hear
Is an important word.
We are becoming more conscious of hearing
What the other person has to.say,
Instead of getting our own point across.
> Usually when we do not hear,
> It is because we are so caught up in our own
> Joy or pain or dullness
>> That we do not even know the other person
>> Has spoken.
>> It is not that we consciously do not hear,
>> But we are preoccupied with trying to find someone
>> Who will hear us.

But if I do not become a listener,
The world may someday run out of them,
And who will hear
Me?

. . . they sold the righteous for silver, and the poor for a pair of shoes. . . .

—Amos 2:6 KJV

*G*ranted
There is no system so profoundly intricate
As the snob system
Of the givers and the receivers.
I may deny myself a pair of shoes
And give them to someone else
Who prefers to go barefoot.

But the fact still remains
That in the face of glaring poverty in the world,
I will go out and buy a pair of shoes
I do not need.

Yet every time I wear those shoes
Will I not wonder
Whose feet
They were intended for?

"Go home to your own folk and tell them what the Lord in his mercy has done for you."

—Mark 5:19 NEB

C oncern . . .
>It conjures up pictures of doe-eyed children
>From other lands,
>Hungry, cold, and under the influence of evil powers.
>>It produces the dime in the collection plate—
>>Or a dollar if we're moved.
>>>Doing good . . .
>>>Some of us find a certain titillation in it
>>>When the good to be done
>>>Is far enough away.

But when I realize that half the good to be done
Is on my street,
Among people with faces like mine,
>Hungry for some honesty,
>Cold, for fear of being warm and human,
>>And under the influence of the sinister power
>>Of keeping up with the Joneses—
What do I do?

*W*hen we hear these words
It is easy to transfer their weight to someone else
Who indulges in profanity,
    Or to shrug off the whole concept
    Of taking God's name in vain as being archaic,
And go on.

But when I view persons
As the faces of God,
These words take on different meaning.
    If I think of myself as a face of God,
    I stand, in a visible way,
    For the creative power in the world.
        I have taken *on* God's name,
        Have assumed a part of his responsibility
        For bringing order and beauty to the world.

Have I taken God's name in vain,
Or am I serious about it?

" 'Love the Lord your God with all your heart, with all your soul, with all your mind. . . . Love your neighbour as yourself.' Everything in the Law and the prophets hangs on these two commandments."

—Matthew 22:37, 38 NEB

God,
    Who is love,
        Love,
            Which accepts,
            Affirms,
            Includes,
            Grows, and builds up,
                Is the creative principle.
But that
    Which rejects,
        Negates,
        Excludes,
        Stagnates,
        And tears down,
        Is the destructive principle.
           It is not love,
                And is the absence of God.

Jesus Christ knew
That acceptance of others
Was the keystone of a creative life.
Do we?

And they were all amazed and perplexed, saying to one another, "What can this mean?" Others said contemptuously, "They have been drinking!"

—Acts 2:12, 13 NEB

*I*n every crowd
There are two kinds of people,
>Those who ask *What does this mean?*
>And those who have the cynical answer.

The people with the ready answers
Have lost their sense of wonder.
All life for them is categorized,
And any new event
Is simply tucked into a category.
>But it is those
>Who, at the risk of being considered naïve,
>Continually ask
>>*What does this mean?*
>>Who sense the true essence of life.

And God made the beast of the earth after his kind, and cattle after their kind, and every thing that creepeth upon the earth after his kind. And God saw that it was good.

—Genesis 1:25 KJV

Little furry kitten
Dozing in a spot of sunlight,
How should I think of you?
    When you open your eyes
    And look at me,
        Do you share the gift of consciousness
        With me?
        The life that is in you,
        Is it the same life that is in me?

        I can hardly conceive of
        The quality of your life
        As being the same as mine . . .
            Is it pure narcissism
            That makes me think
            I and my kind
            Are the only faces of God,
                Or is it true?

Little furry animal
Dozing in a spot of sunlight,
How do you think of yourself?
    Do you dream of a super-cat
    Who made your world
    And view me as a strange uncatly creature?

$\mathcal{M}$ an's essential pride
Seems to make him feel that the spot of the earth
Where he was born, learned to eat, sleep,
Speak, and think,
Was God's natural habitat,
    And that to venture into another location
    Or country,
    Or, God forbid, another culture or social system,
    Is to be in danger of entering the devil's territory.

But how exciting it is,
Once awakened to an awareness
Of the life of God within,
To look into the eyes of people
In the remotest corner of the world
    And discover that there are no remote corners,
    That all points are equidistant from center,
        And to find oneself
        Staring back at oneself,
        Mirrors of this force of God
        Called life.

Looking at people like that
Almost puts the devil out of business.

God is love; and he that dwelleth in love dwelleth in God, and God in him.

—1 John 4:16 KJV

*T*hey told me
That God is love.
    And I forgot
    That love can be fierce,
        That it can strike
        When it is spurned,
            That it can hate
            When it is hurt.

    God is love
    Is not a Sunday-school platitude.
    It claims the motivating force of life
    And centers it in God.

    When I recognize
    God as love,
    I have not simplified anything,
        For the faces of love
        Are as complex as the faces of God,
            And as likely
            To create
            Or destroy.

"Thou hast led in thy steadfast love the people whom thou hast redeemed, thou hast guided them by thy strength to thy holy abode."

—Exodus 15:13 RSV

*T*o come to the moment of awareness,
In all its shining clarity,
Is only a beginning.
>When out of the bondage of my muddled thoughts
>And tangled relationships
>I come to the realization
>>That I am a face of God,
>>That you are a face of God,
>>>That is only the beginning,
>>>A beginning without which
>>>Many other realizations could not come.

But I certainly have not arrived.
If I think I have,
I will simply fall into worse forms of arrogance.
To be aware is only a start.
There is so much to be aware of . . .
>>Like falling in love at first sight,
>>And living together
>>For the next fifty years.

For the Spirit that God has given us does not make us timid; instead, his Spirit fills us with power, love, and self-control.

—2 Timothy 1:7 TEV

$\mathcal{T}$o be a person aware
Of our connection with God
And our fellow man
  Does not mean
  That we must face life with resignation,
  Unconcerned,
  Uninvolved,
  With a give-up-and-let-God attitude.

  Instead,
  The awareness that we are faces of God
  Gives us a tremendous sense of creative power,
  And fills us with love
  For those with whom we share the gift of life.
    It must also give us the self-control
    To handle all that power
    And love,
        And not get all messed up.

Many gave false evidence against him, but their statements did not tally. . . .
But [Jesus] kept silence; he made no reply.

—Mark 14:56, 61 NEB

*T*here are two things
Which cannot be argued against:
Truth
And silence.

When we come to a certain point of awareness,
We discover that whatever can be argued
Is not ultimately true.
The point argued, and its counterpoint,
Are somehow parts of a larger whole.
That whole is what we seek.
And until we find it,
Perhaps silence is the greater wisdom.

So Ananias went. He entered the house, laid his hands on him and said, "Saul, my brother. . . ." And immediately it seemed that scales fell from his eyes, and he regained his sight.

—Acts 9:17, 18 NEB

Just when I become comfortable in thinking
Of people as faces of God,
I encounter a shock . . .

> How can I look on the suffering face
> Of a person dying with cancer,
> And see in him the likeness of God?

> God, is this your face too?
> Do you suffer when we suffer?
> Do you live in us
> Only in good and joyous moments,
> Or do you share our pain?

> Do you care?
> How do I know you care?

God,
Do you care in my caring?
Is the proof of your caring
Contained in the fact that I care?

*. . . a blind beggar . . . began to shout, ". . . Jesus, have pity on me!" Many of
the people told him to hold his tongue.*

—Mark 10:46–48 NEB

Sometimes we have difficulty incorporating trouble
Into our picture of the face of God.
> God is peace and love and goodness,
> He made the birds and trees and flowers,
>> And never mind about who made
>> The spiders, bats and mosquitoes,
>> Rattlesnakes and cancer cells.

When we are engaged in our religious activities,
We are not to think of war and hate, of cruelty and suffering,
As having anything to do with us.
We like to pretend that these things are not shouting at us.
> What would we do if someone stood up
> In the middle of a solemn worship service
> And said, God, I hurt,
> I'm blind and miserable and lonely?

Would we stop the order of worship to hear him—
Or motion for the ushers to take him out?

Is my concept of God
Big enough for my world?
Big enough for pain?

*Remember the days gone by, when, newly enlightened, you met the challenge
. . . and held firm. . . . Do not then throw away your confidence, for it carries a
great reward.*

—Hebrews 10:32, 35 NEB

I remember the first time
My mind came together
And I knew I was a living miracle,
     That the blood coursing through my body
     Was life,
     That the breath in my lungs
     Was life,
     That life was God.
          I remember the day I first came all together—
          I wanted to laugh and sing,
          To throw my arms around a little child
          And dance for the joy of being alive!

I remember . . .
Yet sometimes I face tomorrow with a shudder,
Like an unknowing fool.
          If I have the capacity to remember,
          Should I not also have the capacity to project
          Into the future—
               To project the confidence
               That the same God who has given me
               The miracle of Life
               Will continue to make it of miracle quality?

*I*n our religious life
We can get hung up on such a host of things
    That really have nothing to do
    With the dynamic spirit of faith.
          But if I do not pay attention to detail,
          How will I know when I'm doing it right,
          When I'm succeeding?

Jesus Christ pointed his followers to the birds,
And to the flowers that grew wild in the fields.
That's how it is, he said . . .
    When I can see a flower open
    And feel myself opening,
        When I can see a bird in flight
        And feel that it is somehow flying for me,
          When I as a part of God's creation
          Can feel in touch with my world,
             And live anew
             With every new thing that springs to life,
I can know I'm doing it right.

. . . and these things I will that thou affirm constantly, that they which have believed in God might be careful to maintain good works.

—Titus 3:8 KJV

*T*o remain constant in a world of change
Is both a danger and a necessity.

> There are so many forces pushing
> And pulling at us.
>> The children wonder how we can be so
>> Hopelessly old-fashioned,
>>> And the grandparents wonder how we turned out
>>> So new-fashioned.
>>> The world was fine the way it was—
>>> Why do we have to change everything?

Yet through all the pushing and pulling of the generations,
What really changes?
Nothing much.
Life in its basic longings
Will always turn around to affirm itself,
To preserve itself, to fill up its vacuums.
The basic life of God within us is the great constant.
We change,
To keep that constant alive.

Then Sarai dealt harshly with her.

—Genesis 16:6 RSV

*A*nyone who has read the story of Abraham, Sarai,
And Hagar,
Feels for each person involved.
> What complicated situations we get ourselves into!
> In our impatience to get what we want,
> We use people,
> And when using human beings as things
> Backfires,
> We hate and fear the persons we have used.

It is as old as the Old Testament,
And as new as afternoon soap operas.
But must it go on forever?
If I can be conscious of having God in me,
If I can see my brother as a face of God,
Does the chain of broken relationships need to persist?
> I will try to look into your face and see God there,
> To accept you as good.
> Having accepted you and myself as good,
> Is there any problem we can't work out?

A flower
Is a seed
Is the sun and the earth and the rain . . .

That is true.
      But if I tried to show you a seed,
      And explained about the sun and all the rest,
      Could you imagine a flower?
            The color, the shape, the indescribable perfume?
Never.
Not until you had seen it.
      Like standing on the edge of a new perception
      Of reality
      About God and man.
      One cannot believe it until he has seen it,
         Felt it,
         And shivered at its delight.

Is a flower a seed
      And the sun and the rain?
Yes . . . but no!

O Lord, thou hast searched me, and known me. Thou knowest my downsitting and mine uprising, thou understandest my thought afar off. . . . How precious also are thy thoughts unto me, O God! how great is the sum of them!

—Psalm 139:1, 2, 17 KJV

Sometimes I get so involved in ideas,
In finding meaning in relationships
And human encounters,
    That I am stopped short—
        Have I gone off the track,
        Or gone ahead,
            And left God behind
            In the old ways of thinking and believing?

Then it comes,
Like a cool drink of water on a hot day:
    The awareness that I could not leave him behind,
    That he was the instigator of the idea,
    That he was the idea,
        That he is there in the idea
        Fresh and vital and springing up
        With a strength and clarity
        I never dreamed of.

        Then I know how foolish I am
        To think I could outthink
        God,
            Who goes as far beyond the stretches
            Of my imagination
            As the sky goes beyond the sea.

*W*e like to put up a brave front,
To make a show of strength.
    We wear ourselves out to be strong,
    To be capable,
    To be helpful,
    To do everything
    For other people,
        And we may end up
        Frightening them half to death
        With our efficiency.

Then sometimes it comes by accident,
The crack in the armor . . .
    The shared moment of fear
    Or pain,
    The moment when we stretch out a hand and say
    I too bleed,
    I too cry—
And in relating from weakness
We may reach
What we never could have touched
With our strength.

. . . the faithful God, which keepeth covenant and mercy with them that love him . . . and repayeth them that hate him to their face. . . .

—Deuteronomy 7:9, 10 KJV

*T*he love of God
Is easy to talk about.
It squares well with our concept
Of the creative power.
    But what about the person who hates God,
    Who wants to raise his fist to the sky
    And scream,
        Because life is not a miracle to him,
        Because life is squeezing him
        And trampling him underfoot,
            And there is no reason,
            No answer given for his pain or hunger
            Or loneliness . . .
            Does God punish the person who hates him?

The agony of hating anything
Is its own punishment.
            And when I raise my fist to say
            I hate you,
            There is a kind of cosmic echo that comes back
            And says,
            Hate you.

But echoes are the most easily changed sounds in the world.

". . . I will not revoke the punishment; because they delivered up a whole people, . . . and did not remember the covenant of brotherhood [and sisterhood]."

—Amos 1:9 RSV

*W*hen the list of crimes
A nation
Or a person
Can commit
    Is reduced to one accusation,
    It can be summed up in these words,
    They did not remember the covenant of family.

Perhaps "brotherhood"
Is a worn-out word.
    It reeks of sentimentality,
    Of flowery ideals that got us nowhere
    Except into two world wars . . .
        But have we really understood what it means
        To be brothers and sisters,
        To share genes and noses and eyes
        With those whose faces are a different shape
        And covered with different colors of skin
        From ours?
If we did, would we be so quick to destroy,
Even for a good cause,
Those with whom we share the likeness of God?

*L*ight has a drawing quality.
It makes things grow,
Pulling them up from the ground.
It makes them blossom
And bear fruit.

God's light,
The consciousness of who we are
As faces of God,
Does this for us.
We turn toward our origin
As a plant seeks light,
And we find ourselves being stretched
Upward,
Growing,
Becoming something we were not
With each new day.

Though we have our roots in the earth,
We aspire with our imagination
To touch the sky.

"Men of Athens! I see that in every way you are very religious."

—Acts 17:22 TEV

Ye men of Athens, I perceive that in all things ye are too superstitious.

—Acts 17:22 KJV

*I*n the minds of many thinking people
Religion and superstition have a close affinity.
Is there any difference between the two,
And if so, how can it be expressed?

Religion can be that which gives life unity and purpose,
That which gathers into a rich tapestry
All I hear and see and taste and smell and feel,
And ties them into a miraculous whole of perception
From which there proceeds such a sense of wonder
That anything could happen—
And probably will.

But superstition
Takes that which I do not understand
And explains it in terms
Which contradict my senses and my perception
So that in order to believe it
I must become alienated from life,
And double-minded.

Perhaps the result is not too different,
But the process makes two different kinds of people.

111

You shall remember that you were a slave . . . and the Lord your God redeemed you. . . .

—Deuteronomy 15:15 RSV

*A*fter being freed
From a certain struggle
Or situation,

How easy it is to turn around
And be scornful
Of those who stand where I stood
Only yesterday.

Do I have a friend who is dogmatic,
Who has no questions about life?
        I must remember when I was like that.
Do I have a friend immobilized
By his inability to reconcile
What he thinks he believes
With what he sees around him?
        I must remember when I was like that.

I must remember when I was a slave to a divided heart
And could not see God in my world,
When I thought life was a choice between the two . . .
        And if now I am wiser,
        I should also be kinder.

*If I take the wings of the morning, and dwell in the uttermost parts of the sea;
even there shall thy hand lead me, and thy right hand shall hold me.*

—Psalm 139:9, 10 KJV

*T*here is a fascinating quality in the sea.
It comes and goes
Busily,
Always in ebb or tide,
And yet its basic boundaries never change.

> Constant,
> Changing faces,
> Green and ill at ease in storm,
> Blue and peaceful
> Under a summer sky.

I stand on the edge of the sand
And let the water slip over me.
> Water and salt,
> Motion,
> Sustaining life, and destroying it . . .
> > How are you related to me,
> > Sea?

Someone has set us both in motion,
Has let us both experience change—
> But only within bounds.

Praise him with the sound of the trumpet; praise him with the psaltery and harp.
Praise him with the timbrel and dance; praise him with stringed instruments and
organs.

—Psalm 150:3, 4 KJV

Sometimes I feel
That if I could sing all the songs there are to be sung,
And do all the dances there are to be done
In the front of a church, in a spirit of worship,
I could sort things out better.

>Could I take the words of a popular song,
>Letting every *You* refer to God . . .
>>Not a pristine, stuffy image of God,
>>But God the living, pulsating force of life . . .
>>>And would it have meaning,
>>>Creative meaning?
>>>Then I could sing it to you,
>>>And it would be all right.

>Could I take the steps of a current dance,
>Losing myself in an ecstasy of motion,
>Caught up in the music that pervades the universe,
>Facing you as a face of God,
>And celebrating your being?
>>>Then I could dance this dance with you,
>>>And it would be more than all right.

114

"Give us today our daily bread."

—Matthew 6:11 NEB

J know now
That my life is a miracle,
That to wake up every morning and watch the sun rise,
Or the fog creep,
Or the rain fall,
Is to participate in wonder.

    I know that to have food to eat,
    Clothing for my body,
    And shelter,
    Is enough.
        And that to have meaningful friendships,
        Relationships,
        And responsibilities
        Is more than enough . . .

        Then why am I still so restless?
        What is this strange hunger
        That drives me to discontent,
        That blinds me to the simple goodnesses of life
        And sends me searching for what
        I do not know?
God, help me to taste and smell the fragrance
In a plain loaf of bread.

. . . he knows your going through this great wilderness. . . .

—Deuteronomy 2:7 RSV

*T*he wildernesses we pass through
Are not sand and stone.
They are not trackless treeless plains.
   They are the wildernesses of indecision
   Hung between the if and the but.
      They are the wildernesses
      Of dissatisfaction with ourselves,
      Of hope that we are and fear that we aren't,
      Of being too proud one moment
      And too ashamed the next,
         The wilderness of sticking with routine tasks
         And trying to find some creativity in them.

God,
Do you really have some promised land waiting for me
At the end of this wilderness,
Or have you put me here until I can learn to appreciate
The hues of the desert sand, the cactus flowers,
And the bare wind-swept landscape?
Is this all part of the experience of life, God?
Is this a part of eternity?

"Therefore take good heed to yourselves. Since you saw no form on the day that the Lord spoke to you . . . beware lest you act corruptly by making a graven image for yourselves. . . .

—Deuteronomy 4:15, 16 RSV

Our essential life
Has no form.
It is given to us as fluid, shapeless, creative energy.
You and I could be many things that we are not.

> But necessity drives us to find a niche,
> To take on a name,
> To say *I am a* . . .
> To carve out an identity.

> But I must remember
> That my being, my life,
> Transcends the identity I have chosen.
> I am not basically a teacher or a doctor,
>> A lawyer or a businessman,
>> A parent or a writer.
> Basically, I am a person,
> And should not be bound by ties of status
> Or security
> To any image I have carved out
> As the image of me.
>> I am a part of God,
>> And as such, am a creature of infinite variety.
>> I am free!

For this reason I bow my knees before the Father, from whom every family in heaven and on earth is named. . . .

—Ephesians 3:14, 15 RSV

$\mathcal{I}$ used to think the words of Jesus Christ,
When he turned from his mother and his brothers
And declared the crowd around him to be his family,
     Were cruel and shocking.
Now I think I understand them.

Society is made up of faithfulness
To family
And country.
Without these, social structures crumble.
     But under and over these practical loyalties
     There must be the knowledge
     That all families are one family,
          All countries are one country,
               Under God,
And that when one family or country rises up
To promote its own interests at the expense of another,
There is brokenness
In the family of man . . .
     In the family of God.

Now we see only puzzling reflections in a mirror, but then we shall see face to face.

—1 Corinthians 13:12, 13 NEB

*E*ven with the best of awareness,
How do we see each other now
When you look at me and I look at you?

We see each other as puzzling reflections in a mirror.
    The picture blinks off and on for us . . .
    I can see you as a face of God for a moment,
    And then the picture fades,
    Leaving only your approval or disapproval of me,
        And we are plunged back into the darkness
        Of relating imperfectly.

I know now.
I am aware.
But my awareness is so sporadic.
It is only a glimpse of that state of perfect awareness
Of which I dream.
    And when I reach that day
    When my awareness of God in all his faces
    Is complete and constant,
    That will be heaven.
        No matter where it happens.

Remember where you stand . . . and so worship him as he would be worshipped, with reverence and awe. . . .

—Hebrews 12:18, 28 NEB

𝑅emember where you stand
As an individual whose one unique life
Is of singular value and meaning.

> Remember where you stand,
> A child of parents
> Whose lives are also of singular value and meaning,
> > A parent of children
> > Whose lives may flower into meanings
> > That you will not understand.

> Remember where you stand,
> A member of a community of people,
> A citizen of a country,
> A citizen of the world.
> > Remember where you stand
> > As a container of the Creative Power
> > Of the universe.

Remember where you stand.
Then go and do as you please . . .

> > > with a sense of awe.